Sufism
Mystical writings of Islam

poet in the city

COLLECTORS EDITION

First published in 2007
by Axon Publishing
11 Plough Yard,
London EC2A 3LP

Introduction and Essay
© Poet in the City 2007
Foreword
© Amnesty International 2007
Translations
© individual translators
All rights reserved

Design by Axon Publishing

Reprographics by
EC2i Limited
Southend on Sea
Essex SS2 6UN

Arabic, Persian and Punjabi
typesetting by Papyrus Graphics
papyrusgraphics.com

Printed in Great Britain by
Mayhew McCrimmon
Great Wakering
Southend on Sea
Essex SS3 0PJ

Printed on Emerald Recycled paper

ISBN 978-0-9556113-1-5

Contents

1. PROLOGUE   page 7
   - *Introduction*
   - *Essay*
   - *Foreword*

2. POETRY/PROSE
   Edited and presented by Bruce Wannell

   i. Arabic   page 16-33
   Translations: Ewen Macmillan

   ii. Persian   page 34-53
   Translations: Robert Maxwell
   and Mariam Ma'afi

   iii. Turkish   page 54-57
   Translation: Semra Eren - Nijhar

   iv. Punjabi   page 58-69
   Translations: Richard Harris

3. ACKNOWLEDGMENTS   page 70

poet in the city

COLLECTORS EDITION

PROLOGUE

Introduction

This publication is the record of a live event. These texts in verse or rhymed prose are the record of lived spiritual experience. They are based on the Qur'anic revelation that has nurtured and nourished one of the great mystical traditions – Sufism.

This literature is a by-product or 'spin-off' of the practice of Islam, both as a personal discipline of devotion and piety, and as a public moral action, of the individual questioning despotism, hypocrisy and corruption. The two are closely connected but are not the same – they are conceptually and practically distinct. At its best, the literature inspired by Sufism can give an imaginative entry into the world of lived Islamic mysticism.

Historically, this tradition can be compared to neighbouring and parallel traditions of Eastern Christian Orthodox or Syriac monks and hermits, pagan Turco-mongol bakhshis and shamans, wandering Indian Buddhist monks and Yogi ascetics.

Sufis sought to share their experiences with their local communities by all effective means – with music, singing, folk poetry in the vernacular, and 'high art' poetry in prestige culture languages. While some of the rhetorical conventions and poetic symbols may be unfamiliar, the strength of the lived experience, as in all great art, shines through.

Sufism coloured the classical literatures of the core Islamic languages – Arabic, Persian and Turkish – as well as the languages of the Indian subcontinent. These all contribute today to the vitality of multi-racial, multi-cultural Great Britain, where individual liberty and conscience are respected – and long may this be so.

Bruce Wannell
Editor
- September 2007

How poetry affects our world

Poet in the City is a leading poetry charity that is creating new audiences for poetry and attracting funding into poetry from new sources. Its live poetry events regularly attract audiences of over 250 people, including many who have never previously regarded themselves as poetry fans. Many people say that what they like most about *Poet in the City* is the way in which it makes great poetry accessible, without patronising its audience. It appears that the charity is unlocking a previously unrecognised demand for poetry, and a passionate desire to know more about it. In the process the charity is changing the profile of poetry as an art form, especially amongst corporate sponsors, and is raising substantial sums to pay for poetry education, in particular the placing of poets in state schools.

A very important aspect of *Poet in the City*'s work is the celebration of poetry from around the world. About 20% of the charity's events feature poetry from non-English speaking traditions and cultures. At such events audiences are introduced to the work of some of the world's greatest poets, such as the Chilean poet Pablo Neruda and the Russian poet Anna Akhmatova. Audiences are also introduced to some of the world's richest poetic cultures, from Africa, Asia, Latin America, Eastern Europe and elsewhere. In many of these cultures poetry plays an absolutely vital role, celebrating traditions, challenging authority, or exploring meanings. In many cases we have much to learn from these cultures, both in terms of the exquisite use of language, and the importance and relevance of poetry to society.

At all such events the poetry is performed first in its original language, and then in English translation. The translation of poetry is itself a great art, and the charity works hard to ensure that it uses the very best English translations, versions that convey something of the original magic of the poems. In some ways the separation of the sounds and rhythms from the meanings of the poems can even be advantageous. It forces those who cannot understand the language of the original poems to concentrate, without distraction, on the beauty and musicality of the words before they apprehend their meaning from the translation that follows.

In September 2006 *Poet in the City* held a Sufism event at the UK Headquarters of Amnesty International in Shoreditch. This was one of a series of successful poetry events that *Poet in the City* has held jointly with Amnesty over the last few years. It is a great pleasure to work with such an important campaigning organisation, which brings great commitment and professionalism to these collaborations. It is also an excellent way of demonstrating that poetry is not something that is merely of literary or academic interest, but is a living force, capable of speaking about some of the world's most pressing issues.

Whenever *Poet in the City* works with Amnesty International the invitation to the poetry event is accompanied by an Action Card highlighting current human rights abuses around the world. In the case of the Sufism event this concerned the plight of 52 Nematollahi Sufis and their lawyers, beaten and imprisoned in Iran for holding a peaceful protest against the closure of their place of worship. It is hard to think of a more eloquent expression of the way in which Sufism and its ideas are relevant to the current battle being waged for the traditions of Islam.

> A rich cultural heritage that emphasises the common humanity which unites us all

The event was also supported by the Department of Local Government and Communities. This was, after all, an event that was promoting some of the marvels of Islamic culture to an audience that included both Muslims and non-Muslims, and a rich cultural heritage that emphasises the common humanity which unites us all. In the aftermath of the 7/7 bombings in London this seemed a particularly important message to convey. As if to confirm the importance of this, a week or two before the event it was announced that a Sufi Muslim Council was being launched in the UK with the express purpose of condemning extremism and championing the more tolerant and inclusive traditions within Islam. Never did a poetry event feel more timely or appropriate.

PROLOGUE

The Sufism event was, without doubt, one of the best events ever held by *Poet in the City*. It was one of those life-changing occasions on which your eyes are opened to the inestimable riches of another culture and tradition. In this case the poems, some of which dated back to the 10th Century, were astonishing not only for the intricate beauty of their sounds and rhythms, but also for their spiritual resonance and their topicality. They raise questions about the meaning of life and death, about our desires and yearnings, and about the need for tolerance and peace, which are just as relevant now as on the day they were written.

Bruce Wannell, who has dedicated his life to the study of Islamic culture, was the perfect person to introduce Sufism and to place its poetry in context. He gave us a brief tour through the Islamic world, from the Arabian peninsular to Turkey, from Egypt and Persia to the Punjab. The poems themselves were read in their original languages by a series of readers including Aladdin Ahmed and Shihab al-Ahwazi (Arabic), Abbas Faiz and Maryam Hashemi (Farsi), Semra Eren-Nijhar (Turkish) and Anita Mir and Amarjit Chandan (Punjabi). They were also read in English translation by Robert Maxwell and Ewen Macmillan. The evening concluded with an hour of Sufi music from the celebrated percussionist Yusuf Mahmoud (tabla), accompanied by John Baily (rubâb), Veronica Doubleday (dâ'ira) and the Afghan singer Timor Shaidaie. Those present experienced an amazing musical feast, closely connected to the spirit of the Sufi poetry that had gone before.

> The poems raise questions which are just as relevant now as on the day they were written

Poet in the City is privileged to have many of its events recorded for posterity by the British Library Sound Archive. Those who wish to hear the original Sufism event from September 2006 in its entirety can do so by arrangement with the Library, where a full recording forms part of the resources of the Sound Archive, a truly amazing collection that contains this and many other precious recordings, carefully preserved on behalf of the nation.

No single *Poet in the City* event has ever aroused so much interest and enthusiasm. Many of the audience left with a strong desire to learn more about Sufism, its great philosophical insights and its extraordinary artistic achievements. At a time when Islamic culture was often being portrayed by the media in a stereotypical or one-dimensional way, the event showed it in a very different light: aesthetic, sophisticated, nuanced, self-questioning and profound. It was clear right away that the event constituted an excellent introduction to the subject of mystical Islam, and that the poetry it featured was a marvellous way into the subject. Bruce Wannell and I agreed that it would be a good idea to publish the poetry featured in the event.

Thanks to the generous sponsorship of Axon Publishing we are now able to do so, and to introduce a selection of some of the beautiful writings of the Sufis to a wider audience. I would like to thank Paul Keers and Ellen Brush and their colleagues at Axon Publishing for making this lovely publication possible. Unlike the original event, on which it is based, this publication also presents to the reader the beautiful scripts of the original Arabic, Persian and Punjabi poems. I would especially like to congratulate Amar Hussain of Axon, winner of Young Designer of the Year 2007, for his beautiful design. I know that this has been a project very close to his heart.

Special thanks should also go to Amnesty for supporting the Sufism event, and for endorsing this publication. In particular I would like to thank Alison Willis, Nicky Parker and Maggie Paterson. *Poet in the City* looks forward to other such collaborations with Amnesty International in support of its invaluable work in defence of human rights all over the world.

We have also benefited from help with the Punjabi translations here from Richard Harris, former head of the BBC World Service Indian section. Last, but by no means least, publication would not have been possible without the energy and expertise of Bruce Wannell, who has acted as its editor and prime mover. The success of the original event was largely due to his knowledge and his skilful selection of poems and readers. *Poet in the City*, Axon Publishing and Amnesty International have relied heavily upon his talent and dedication.

> Reading and listening to Sufi poetry has opened my eyes to a different tradition

Reading and listening to Sufi poetry has opened my eyes to a different tradition. I hope that this collectors' edition gives you as much pleasure as it has given me, and that it inspires and stimulates you in the way that only great and important poetry can.

Graham Henderson
Chief Executive
Poet in the City
- September 2007

Foreword by Amnesty International

Poetry is unique to humankind; the capacity to create and enjoy poetry lies within us all. It is sometimes seen as achievable only at the pinnacle of civilization, yet many people have recourse to poetry at times of extreme hardship. Poetry is a calling out of the human spirit to express itself with truth; it is the burning of an irrepressible flame of human creativity.

There is something else about the act of creating poetry that has a deep resonance with the work of Amnesty International: it is as powerful an assertion of human dignity as you can hope to find. Despite repression, despite torture, individuals all over the world take extraordinary comfort from reading and writing poetry. It is a laying bare of the soul in a form of personal expression that can soar above appalling hardship. It has the strength to sustain the human psyche.

Sufism is the mystical branch of Islam, whose poets write ecstatically of their relationship with the divine. The poets in this collection are long dead, but their words live on, a testament to the enduring power of poetry to touch others.

The poems in this anthology are beautiful, personal acts of creation. When you read them, it seems extraordinary that the faith of their creators should be under threat. Yet Amnesty International researchers report alarming attacks on Sufis in Iran and Bangladesh in the last couple of years. In 2006, for example, over 1,000 Nematollahi Sufis were arrested in Iran. They were peacefully protesting against an order to evacuate their place of worship – their protest included offering white flowers and cake to local residents. Hundreds were injured by the security forces and organised pro-government groups. In May, 52 of them were sentenced to one year's imprisonment, flogging and a fine, and their lawyers were banned from practising law. In August, Grand Ayatollah Fazel Lankarani issued a religious edict designating Sufism 'null and void'.

It is a sad truth that many of us have a deep fear of those who believe in a different path. And our fear turns too often to violence and repression. For thousands of years people have been tortured, imprisoned and killed on the basis of their religious beliefs. Yet for many of the poets in this anthology, unity with the divine is beyond earthly cultural limitations.

We at Amnesty International have a term for those imprisoned for their beliefs: 'prisoners of conscience'. This was coined in 1961, when British lawyer Peter Benenson read about two Portuguese students who were sentenced to seven years' imprisonment simply for raising a toast to freedom. He wrote to the *Observer*, calling for an international campaign to bombard authorities around the world with protests about 'prisoners of conscience'. The appeal received a tremendous response. Today, nearly half a century on, Amnesty International has grown into a global movement with over two million supporters. Our vision is of a world in which everybody enjoys all the human rights enshrined in the Universal Declaration of Human Rights. As we have grown, our focus has expanded to take in not just prisoners of conscience, but other victims of human rights abuses – such as torture, 'disappearances' and the death penalty – throughout the world.

'Everyone has the right to freedom of thought, conscience and religion'

'Everyone has the right to freedom of opinion and expression'

UNIVERSAL DECLARATION OF HUMAN RIGHTS (UDHR), ARTICLES 18 AND 19

The inspired poetry in this volume speaks more than it knows about the iniquity of censorship and repression. We can all do something to speak out on behalf of those suffering terrible violations of their human rights. Please find out what you can do to make a difference – we at Amnesty International will be glad to help.

Kate Allen
Director
Amnesty International UK
www.amnesty.org.uk
- September 2007

Arabic

The number of Arabic speakers has been estimated between 246 million and 422 million; it is the most widespread of the Semitic language family including Hebrew, Syriac and Ethiopic. The scripts are derived from Aramaic or old South Arabian, and enshrine the holy books of the Jews (the Torah), the eastern Christians (Gospels of the 4 Evangelists etc) and of the Muslims (the Qur'an). The Arab Muslim conquests of the early 7th century established Arabic as the imperial language of a community that stretched from Spain to Central Asia and Sindh in India, with Islam as the official religion and the Qur'an as its central text. Later conquests took Islam further into India, Byzantine Anatolia and the Balkans, while traders proselytised peacefully along the shores of the western Indian Ocean and as far as Indonesia, right up to the period of European colonialism.

THE HOLY QUR'AN

The Qur'an, the fundamental text of Islam, has provided the standard of literary Arabic and the source of personal religious experience and meditation from the beginning of the Islamic era. The passage quoted dates from before the 'Hijra' of 622; Muhammad responds to the troubling vision of the Archangel Gabriel bringing him the revelation, with all that it implied of radically turning his life around from being a private merchant to becoming a public Prophet.

MANSUR AL-HALLAJ

From the 8th to the 13th centuries, personal piety and devotion became important to revive the spirit of an increasingly legalistic official religion. One of the wilder students of this movement was Mansur al-Hallaj, from Baghdad, executed in 922 for his apparently blasphemous ecstatic utterance 'I am the Truth'. A sub-category of Sufi expression is these 'shathiyyat', shocking paradoxes that yet express a moment of the spiritual reality of self-transcendence.

AL-NIFFARI

Another Iraqi mystic of the mid-10th century from the ancient Babylonian city of Nippur presents surreal visions, here the near experience of death where all humanity is stripped away, and only

God's mercy re-establishes the quality of being human. This is an experience no doubt shared by prisoners of conscience and victims of torture anywhere.

IBN SINA

This great scholar of medicine and natural science, better known as Avicenna, was born near Bukhara, where he studied under the rule of the 10th century Persian Samanids. Political turbulence forced him to migrate ever westwards, composing his works as he went. He died in Hamadan in western Iran. In his last book, he included his more personal philosophy tinged with Sufism, including this magnificent definition of the courage and generosity characteristic of all truly independent intellectuals and mystics.

IBN ARABI

Many Spanish Muslim mystics and writers migrated east during the centuries of the Catholic 'reconquista'. Muhiy-al-Din ibn 'Arabi was born in Murcia and died in Damascus. During his pilgrimage to Mecca he met a learned lady, Nizam of Isfahan, who inspired this collection of mystical love poems written in 1214, where love both human and divine revives the heart. In Arabic 'qalb', the heart, comes from the same verbal root as 'qalaba' to turn or change, thus reflecting its changing qualities. In the lines quoted, the mystic's and lover's heart rises above the narrow confessional definitions that constrict being into mutually hostile identities – surely a lesson that Sufism can give to the world, even today.

AL-FARID

The great poet 'Umar ibn al-Farid drew on the rhetorical conventions and symbols of secular Arabic love and wine poetry to express mystical insights. This poem declares his intense love for the person of the Prophet Muhammad, and was inspired by meeting Shihab al-Din Suhrawardi, the influential Sufi from Baghdad, during the pilgrimage to Mecca in 1231. The poem remains a favourite with the 'munshidin' singers of Egypt – the links between poetry and song remain fundamental to the oral culture of the Islamic world.

IBN ATAULLAH

Ibn Ataullah of Alexandria died in Cairo, where he helped establish the confraternity of the Shadhiliyya – a movement of organised mysticism corresponding to similar developments elsewhere in Islam, parallel to the orders of monks and friars in medieval Catholic Europe. His collection of spiritual aphorisms in lucid and luminous style is based on a subtle psychology characteristic of Sufism. The incantatory repetitions aim to explore the paradox of immanence and transcendence of the divine in all creation.

In the name of Allah, Most Gracious, Most Merciful

1. By the Star when it goes down,
2. Your Companion is neither astray nor being misled.
3. Nor does he say (aught) of (his own) Desire.
4. It is no less than inspiration sent down to him:
5. He was taught by one Mighty in Power,
6. Endued with Wisdom: for he appeared (in stately form);
7. While he was in the highest part of the horizon:
8. Then he approached and came closer,
9. And was at a distance of but two bow-lengths or (even) nearer;
10. So did (Allah) convey the inspiration to His Servant (conveyed) what He (meant) to convey.
11. The (Prophet's) (mind and) heart in no way falsified that which he saw.
12. Will ye then dispute with him concerning what he saw?
13. For indeed he saw him at a second descent,
14. Near the Lote-tree beyond which none may pass:
15. Near it is the Garden of Abode.
16. Behold, the Lote-tree was shrouded (in mystery unspeakable!)
17. (His) sight never swerved, nor did it go wrong!
18. For truly did he see, of the Signs of his Lord, the Greatest!

QUR'AN, SURA AL-NAJM, AYA 1 – 18, (BEFORE 622)

NOTES:

English translation of the text meanings and Commentary from King Fahd Holy Qur'an printing Complex, Al-Madinah Al-Munawarah under the Auspices of the Ministry of Hajj and Endowments. The Kingdom of Saudi Arabia. Pages 1636-1638.

ARABIC: THE HOLY QUR'AN

بِسْمِ ٱللَّهِ ٱلرَّحْمَٰنِ ٱلرَّحِيمِ

وَٱلنَّجْمِ إِذَا هَوَىٰ ۝

مَا ضَلَّ صَاحِبُكُمْ وَمَا غَوَىٰ ۝

وَمَا يَنطِقُ عَنِ ٱلْهَوَىٰٓ ۝

إِنْ هُوَ إِلَّا وَحْيٌ يُوحَىٰ ۝

عَلَّمَهُۥ شَدِيدُ ٱلْقُوَىٰ ۝

ذُو مِرَّةٍ فَٱسْتَوَىٰ ۝

وَهُوَ بِٱلْأُفُقِ ٱلْأَعْلَىٰ ۝

ثُمَّ دَنَا فَتَدَلَّىٰ ۝

فَكَانَ قَابَ قَوْسَيْنِ أَوْ أَدْنَىٰ ۝

فَأَوْحَىٰٓ إِلَىٰ عَبْدِهِۦ مَآ أَوْحَىٰ ۝

مَا كَذَبَ ٱلْفُؤَادُ مَا رَأَىٰٓ ۝

أَفَتُمَٰرُونَهُۥ عَلَىٰ مَا يَرَىٰ ۝

وَلَقَدْ رَءَاهُ نَزْلَةً أُخْرَىٰ ۝

عِندَ سِدْرَةِ ٱلْمُنتَهَىٰ ۝

عِندَهَا جَنَّةُ ٱلْمَأْوَىٰٓ ۝

إِذْ يَغْشَى ٱلسِّدْرَةَ مَا يَغْشَىٰ ۝

مَا زَاغَ ٱلْبَصَرُ وَمَا طَغَىٰ ۝

لَقَدْ رَأَىٰ مِنْ ءَايَٰتِ رَبِّهِ ٱلْكُبْرَىٰٓ ۝

Sufism 19

I am the Truth

MANSUR AL-HALLAJ (DIED 922)

ARABIC: MANSUR AL-HALLAJ

أنا الحقّ

He stopped me in Death.
And I saw   deeds, every one of them as evil
             fear, domineering over hope
             wealth, turned to fire, becoming one with fire
             poverty, a hostile witness
             everything, incapable of anything
             this world, as vanity
             the heavens, as deception.
I cried out 'Science?!' No answer.
I cried out 'Intuition?!' No answer.

I saw everything had deserted me, every creature had fled from me.
I was left quite alone.

Deeds came to me and I saw in them hidden illusion, that turned to dust.

There was no help except the mercy of my Lord.
He said to me   'Where is your science?' I saw the fire.
                 'Where are your deeds?' I saw the fire.
                 'Where is your intuition?' I saw the fire.
And He unveiled to me His unique sources of knowing. So the fire died down.
He said to me   'I am your protector and friend!' So I stood firm.
                 'I am your intuition!' So I spoke out.
                 'I want you!' So I went forth.

AL-NIFFARI (CIRCA 966)
KITAB AL-MAWAQIF

ARABIC: AL-NIFFARI

أوقفني في الموت فرأيت الأعمال كلها ميتات ورأيت الخوف يتحكم على الرجاء ورأيت الغنى قد صار ناراً ولحق بالنار ورأيت الفقر خصماً يحتج ورأيت كل شيءٍ لا يقدر على شيءٍ ورأيت الملك غروراً ورأيت الملكوت خداعاً

وناديت يا علمُ فلم يجبني وناديت يا معرفةُ فلم تجبني ورأيت كل شيءٍ قد أسلمني ورأيت كل خليقةٍ قد هرب مني وبقيت وحدي

وجاءني العمل فرأيت فيه الوهم الخفي والخفي الغابر

فما نفعني ألا رحمة ربي

وقال لي أين عملك فرأيت النار

وقال لي أين معرفتك فرأيت النار

وكشف لي عن معارفه الفردانية فخمدت النار

وقال لي أنا وليك فثبت

وقال لي أنا معرفتك فنطقت

وقال لي أنا طالبك فخرجت

Sufism 23

One who knows spiritual truth is courageous:
> how not?
>> for he goes beyond fear of death.

He is generous:
> how not?
>> for he goes beyond a vain love of passing things.

He is forgiving of others' faults:
> how not?
>> for his inner self is too great to be wounded by others.

He is forgetful of slights and injuries:
> how not?
>> for his consciousness is wholly occupied by divine Truth.

IBN SINA (DIED 1037)
KITAB AL-ISHARAT WA AL-TANBIHAT

ARABIC: **IBN SINA**

العارفُ شجاعٌ وكيفَ لا
وَهُوَ بمعزلٍ عن تقيةِ الموتِ
فجوادٌ وكيفَ لا
وَهُوَ بمعزلٍ عن مَحَبةِ الباطلِ
وَصفاحٌ للذنُوبِ وكيفَ لا
ونفسُه أكبرُ من أن تجرحها ذاتُ بشرٍ
ونسّاءٌ للأحقادِ وكيفَ لا
وذِكرُه مشغولٌ بالحقِ

'Incredible! A garden among fires,
My heart turns to all forms,
It has become   a meadow where gazelles graze
                    a monastery where monks pray;
                    a temple for idol statues
                    a cube for circumambulating pilgrims;
                    both Torah scroll and bound volume of Qur'an.
I follow the religion of love:
        where love's camels lead, there is my religion and there my faith.'

IBN ARABI (DIED 1240)
TARJUMAN AL-ASHWAQ

NOTES:
Torah - Hebrew Scripture
Qur'an - Muslim 'reading', Holy Book

ARABIC: IBN ARABI

ويا عجباً من روضةٍ وسطَ نيرانِ

لقد صارَ قلبي قابلاً كلَّ صورةٍ   فمرعىً لِغزلانٍ وديرٌ لرهبانِ

وبيتٌ لأوثانٍ وكعبةُ طائفٍ   وألواحُ توراةٍ ومصحفُ قرآنِ

أدينُ بدينِ الحبِّ أنى توجهت   ركائبهُ فالدينُ ديني وإيماني

In the middle of battle where looks and hearts engage,
    see, I am slain, with no trouble nor guilt.
Before passion was, I said farewell to my soul, for my eyes have seen
    that vision of radiant loveliness.
O God, these eyelids sleepless for you,
    yearning for you, heart anguished for you!
Welcome sickness for you, which makes me invisible to myself,
    there stand my proofs for love of you.
I wake troubled at morning, as at night
    yet I never cry out impatiently, 'O pain, go away!'
Punish me however you will, but not with banishment from you, and you
    will find a most loyal lover, whatever satisfies you makes me joyful.
Take what little life-breath you have left me:
    It is a useless love that allows souls to subsist.
Who dies in love for Him, lives ever praised
    among the passionate, to the highest degree.
Though I wander lost in the black hair of night,
    yet the white forehead of dawn guides my sight.
The Divine turns towards me in years brief as day,
    but turns away in days endless as years.
And if He travels far away, O my heart go too!
    and if He comes near to visit me, then O my eyes rejoice!
O you of tranquil heart, do not look to my comforter,
    master your own heart, beware his riotous dark eyes!
O my companion, I am gracious and kind
    I have scattered the seed of advice: go not aside to that quarter!
God bless the one I love and His sweet character!
    how many hearts have died and come back to life because of Him!
Though He is hidden from me, yet each element of my being sees Him
    in each subtle sense, grace and joy,
In plucked songs of the lute and mellifluous flute
    When they mingle in the Hazaj mode,

/CONTINUED OVERLEAF

ما بَينَ مُعَنِّرِكِ الأحداقِ والمُهَج	أنا القتيلُ بلا إثمٍ ولا حَرَج
ودّعتُ قبلَ الهوى روحي لما نظرت	عيناي من حُسنِ ذاك المنظرِ البَهِج
للَّهِ أجفانُ عينٍ فيك ساهرةً	شوقاً إليك وقلبٌ بالغرامِ شَج
وحبّذا فيك أسقامٌ خفيتُ بها	عني تقومُها عند الهوى حُجَجي
أصبحتُ فيك كما أمسيتُ مكتئباً	ولم أقل جزعاً: يا أزمةَ انفرجي
عذِّب بما شئتَ غيرَ البُعدِ عنك نجد	أوفى محبٍّ بما يُرضيك مُبتهِج
وخُذ بقيةَ ما أبقيتَ من رمَقي	لا خيرَ في الحبِّ إن أبقى على المُهَج
مَن مات فيه غراماً عاش مُرتقياً	ما بين أهلِ الهوى في أرفعِ الدَّرَج
وإن ضَلَلتُ بليلٍ من ذوائبه	أهدى لعيني الهدى صبحٌ من البَلَج
أعوامُ إقبالِه كاليومِ في قِصَر	ويومُ إعراضِه في الطولِ كالحُجَج
فإن نأى سائراً يا مُهجتي ارتحلي	وإن دنا زائراً يا مقلتي ابتهجي
يا ساكنَ القلبِ لا تنظر إلى سكني	واريِّح فؤادك واحذر فتنةَ الدَّعَج
يا صاحبي وأنا البَرُّ الرؤوفُ وقد	بذلتُ نصحي بذاك الحيِّ لا تَعُج
تباركَ اللَّهُ ما أحلى شمائلَه	فكم أماتت وأحيَت فيه من مُهَج
تراهُ إن غاب عني كلُّ جارحةٍ	في كلِّ معنى لطيفٍ رائقٍ بَهِج
في نغمةِ العودِ والنايِ الرخيمِ إذا	تآلفا بين ألحانٍ من الهَزَج

In meadows where gazelles graze
>   in cool evening or at earliest dawn,
In dews falling gently from the clouds
>   on a lawn woven of flowers,
In breezes trailing skirts wafting
>   at dawn their sweetest perfumes to me,
In kisses on the mouth of the cup sucking
>   fragrant wine in a blissful shade:
If He be with me, I know not what it is to be far from home:
>   wherever we are, my mind is wholly untroubled.
For that home is my home where my love is present, when He is manifest
>   to me, climbing the steep hill is also my ascension.

AL-FARID (DIED 1235)
DIWAN

NOTES:
Hazaj - Arabic rhythmic mode or poetic metre used for cheerful melodies

ARABIC: AL-FARID

وفي مَسارحِ غِزلانِ الحمائلِ   في بَرْدِ الأصائلِ والإصباحِ في البَلَجِ
وفـي مَساقِطِ أنـداءِ الغَمامِ   على بِساطٍ نَورٍ مِنَ الأزهارِ مُنْسَجِ
وفي مَساحِبِ أذيالِ النسيمِ   إذا أهدى إليّ سُحَيراً أطيَبَ الأرَجِ
وفي النِّتامي ثَغَرَ الكأسِ مُرتَشِفاً   رِيقَ المُدامةِ في مُستَنزَهٍ فَرِجِ
لمرَ أدرِ ما غُربَةُ الأوطانِ وهو معي   وخاطِري أينَ كنّا غيرُ مُنزَعِجِ
فالدارُ داري وحُبّي حاضرٌ ومُنى   بدا فمُنعَرَجُ الجَرعاءِ مُنعَرَجي

Hear the proofs of His all-conquering power:
>One of them is that He veils himself from you by things which do not really exist
>
>because He is the only real existent.

How can it be imagined that something could veil Him,
>He who unveils all things, who is unveiled in all things by all things,
>
>He who is unveiled to all things before all things,
>
>how could anything veil Him?

Why do you think that He might be veiled?
>He is more manifest than anything.
>
>He is the unique. Nothing exists except Him.

How could anything veil Him? He is closer to you than anything.

What thing could possibly veil Him? Without Him nothing would exist.

O mystery of Being, appearing in the void of nothingness,
>that the temporal should subsist in the presence of God
>>whose attribute is Eternity.

IBN ATAULLAH (DIED 1309)
KITAB AL-HIKAM

ARABIC: IBN ATAULLAH

مِما يَدُلُّك على وُجُودِ قَهرِهِ سبحانه
أَن حَجَبَك عنه بِما ليس بِموجودٍ معه

كَيفَ يُنصورُ أَن يحجبهُ شيءٌ
وَهُوَ الذي أَظهَرَ كُلَّ شيءٍ

كَيفَ يُنصورُ أَن يحجبهُ شيءٌ
وَهُوَ الذي ظَهَرَ بِكُلِّ شيءٍ

كَيفَ يُنصورُ أَن يحجبهُ شيءٌ
وَهُوَ الذي ظَهَرَ في كُلِّ شيءٍ

كَيفَ يُنصورُ أَن يحجبهُ شيءٌ
وَهُوَ الذي ظَهَرَ لِكُلِّ شيءٍ

كَيفَ يُنصورُ أَن يحجبهُ شيءٌ
وَهُوَ الظاهرُ قَبلَ وجودِ كُلِّ شيءٍ

كَيفَ يُنصورُ أَن يحجبهُ شيءٌ
وَهُوَ أَظهَرُ مِن كُلِّ شيءٍ

كَيفَ يُنصورُ أَن يحجبهُ شيءٌ
وَهُوَ الواحدُ الذي ليسَ مَعَهُ شيءٌ

كَيفَ يُنصورُ أَن يحجبهُ شيءٌ
وَهُوَ أَقرَبُ إِليكَ مِن كُلِّ شيءٍ

كَيفَ يُنصورُ أَن يحجبهُ شيءٌ
وَلَولاهُ لَما كانَ وُجُودُ كُلِّ شيءٍ

يا عَجَباً كيفَ يظهرُ الوجودُ في العَدَمِ
أَم كيفَ يثبتُ الحادثُ مع من لهُ وصفُ القِدَمِ

Persian

Persian, one of the most anciently attested Indo-European languages, is spoken by an estimated 50 to 100 million people, in the area stretching from the Euphrates River to the oasis cities of Central Asia and the Pamir Mountains, with its heartland on the Iranian plateau and its south-western province of Fars. Old Persian was the language of the great multi-cultural empire of the 5th century BC Achaemenids, who also used Aramaic as the imperial language of administration and trade. The Sasanians ruled from Ctesiphon near Baghdad from the 3rd century AD and their empire, middle Persian in language, Zoroastrian in faith, stretched from the Mediterranean to the borders of China and India. Military defeat by the Muslim Arabs in 652 led to a temporary eclipse, until it re-emerged as the cultural language of the Islamic Samanid dynasty of Bukhara in the 10th century. It kept this role as the prestige culture language of Islam under the subsequent dynasties of Turkish origin, right up till the 19th century, under the Mughals in India and the Ottomans in Anatolia and around the Mediterranean.

Abdullah Ansari

'Abdullah Ansari was of Arab descent, Persian in culture. He was a strict Hanbali, intransigent in legal observance, which led to his temporary exile. His 'intimate conversations with God' based on his bold personal relationship with the Divine, are in rhyming prose and quatrains, forms used for improvised and sung folk poetry and used by Sufis in reaching out to all social classes. The book remains one of the most widely read works of personal piety in the Persian speaking Muslim world.

Rumi

Jalal al-Din Rumi's family originated in Balkh in northern Afghanistan, but migrated west, fleeing the Mongol invasions, to Konya in Anatolia. Rumi studied there and in Syria, and taught as a respected scholar, until his meeting with a wandering dervish, Shams al-Din of Tabriz, gave him the psychological shock that transformed him into one of the greatest love mystics of the Sufi tradition. The first poem quoted, using incantatory repetitions, explores the psychology of self-obsession contrasted with self-transcendence. A brief quatrain follows, which encapsulates the moment of grasping timelessness in what are known as 'integrated states'. The poem to his dying disciple and son-in-law merges the human love with love of the Prophet and love of God, culminating in the acceptance of renunciation and loss.

Muslih al-Din Sa'di

Muslih al-Din Sa'di came from, and returned to, Shiraz, the capital city of Fars in the Muslim period. He studied in Baghdad, shortly before its destruction by the Mongols in 1258, and subsequently travelled widely, gathering the anecdotal experiences that enliven his books of didactic wisdom. He also perfected the Persian 'ghazal' short ode, of which the example here marries the dancing rhythms of the metre with the joy felt in creation as a mirror of the Divine creator.

Shams-al-Din Muhammad Hafez

Also of Shiraz, Shams-al-Din Muhammad Hafez took the Persian 'ghazal' to new heights of subtlety and lyric beauty, marrying courtly and mystical traditions, with even some political asides, as in those poems referring to the conquests of Timur the Lame, whom he is said to have met shortly before his death in 1389. The poem quoted here, based on the legend of Joseph and his grieving father Jacob in Canaan, has been a promise and source of consolation to Persian speakers world-wide, who often take 'fal' omens from his Divan of poetry.

Abdul Qader Bidel

'Abdul Qader Bidel was the greatest exponent of the complex and mannered Indian style of the Persian ghazal. He lived and died in Delhi under Aurangzeb, the last of the really powerful Moghul emperors, and absorbed not only the great classical tradition of Persian poetry and Islamic mysticism, but also elements of Hindu philosophy and scepticism. Here he re-asserts the fundamental Islamic teaching that the creature remains separate from his Creator, whom he venerates and worships. True self-transcendence is not the sometimes facile and self-indulgent claim of ecstatics to be able to communicate directly with the Divine: illusion and vanity are to be detected even in the most enthusiastic spiritual states.

You, who have made us without charge
And feed us with generosity,
Forgive us with an equally open heart:
You are God, who does not act commercially.

I am nothing but a disobedient slave,
So how can you be satisfied with me?
My heart is darkly black, and where
Is your light that should be blazing out from me?

But if your grant of Paradise depends
On my obeying all your just commands,
That's no more than contractually fair.
Where then is your liberality?

ABDULLAH ANSARI (DIED 1088)
MUNAJAT

PERSIAN: ABDULLAH ANSARI

الهی
آفریدی رایگان
و روزی   دادی رایگان
بیامرز رایگان
که تو خدائی   نه بازارگان
من بندهِ عاصیم: رضایِ تو کجاست؟
تاریک دِلم: نور و ضیایِ تو کجاست؟
مارا تو بهشت اگر بطاعت بخشی
آب بیع بود: لطف و عطایِ تو کجاست؟

That moment's breath when you are self-obsessed,
your beloved is no more welcome than a thorn,
Yet when you have left selfishness behind,
    what use to you is your beloved then?

That moment's breath when you are self-obsessed,
mosquitos hunt you down,
Yet when you have left selfishness behind,
    you can hunt elephants.

That moment's breath when you are self-obsessed,
you are imprisoned in a fog of grief,
Yet when you have left selfishness behind,
    the moon itself comes willing to you then.

That moment's breath when you are self-obsessed,
your love will hide itself away,
Yet when you have left selfishness behind,
    The ecstasy of love comes to you then.

That moment's breath when you are self-obsessed,
you are as frozen as the autumn frost,
Yet when you have left selfishness behind,
    Winter is like spring-time to you then.

Your rootlessness comes from your seeking rootedness,
    Become an unresting seeker, and you will have true firmness then.

All your allergies are from eating faddish foods,
    Stop seeking what is easy: even poison will not harm you then.

All your frustrations stem from attempts to please yourself,
    Stop the search: your wishes will be showered on you then.

Love your love for his harshness, not his generous gifts,
    His teasing beauty will come humbly to you then.

When the King of East, the Son of Faith, Shams ud-Din comes
    By God, all other moons and stars will have faded then.

RUMI (DIED 1273)
DIVAN SHAMS TABRIZI

NOTES:
Shams ud-Din - Literally 'Sun of Religion', Rumi's Sufi master and inspiration

آن نفسی که با خودی یار چو خار آیدت

وان نفسی که بی خودی، یار چه کار آیدت

آن نفسی که با خودی، خود تو شکار پشه ای

وان نفسی که بی خودی، پیل شکار آیدت

آن نفسی که با خودی، بسته ی ابر غصّه ای

وان نفسی که بی خودی، مه به کنار آیدت

آن نفسی که با خودی، یار کناره می کند

وان نفسی که بی خودی، باده ی یار آیدت

آن نفسی که با خودی همچو خزان فسرده ای

وان نفسی که بی خودی، دی چو بهار آیدت

جمله ی بی قراریت از طلب قرار تست

طالب بی قرار شو تا که قرار آیدت

جمله ی ناگوارشت از طلب گوارش است

ترک گوارش ار کنی، زهر گوار آیدت

جمله ی بی مرادیت از طلب مراد تست

ور نه همه مرادها همچو نثار آیدت

عاشق جور یار شو، عاشق مهر یار نی

تا که نگار نازگر: عاشق زار آیدت

خسرو شرق شمس دین، از تبریز چون رسد

از مه و از ستاره ها – والله – عار آیدت

When I become the Sea
each atom flames out of me in glory.
When I am ablaze
each moment becomes Eternity.

RUMI (DIED 1273)
TRANSLATED BY MARIAM MA'AFI

PERSIAN: RUMI

آنوقت که بحرِ کلّ شود ذات مرا

روشن گردد جهانِ ذرّات مرا

زان میسوزم چو شمع تا در رهِ عشق

یک وقت شود جملهءِ اوقات مرا

Veiled like the soul, making me whole
You enter my heart.
Elegant as a tree, delighting me,
You stand apart. Slender and tall, high overall
With a garden's art.

Do not leave me alone, when you have gone
Soul of my soul.
Leave not body behind, springing free but unkind
Flame without coal. Leave not my sight, take not my light,
Break not the whole.

I plunder the skies, take stars as my prize
When I know your love,
I pass through the seas, fearless, with ease
With hand in your glove. You make my head spin, dizzy within
From the eyes of your love.

I fear not faith, nor yet unbelief
Since you entered my arms,
Seeing you is my creed, my lodestar in need
My talisman from harm. Your sight is my stay, my celestial way,
In every alarm.

I am helpless, clumsy and witless
Since you made me your own.
I cannot eat, nor function, nor sleep
Since you joined bone to bone. Come Joseph my son, beloved one
To Canaan's home.

By your gift, your holy shrift
I become like the soul.
Hidden even from myself, absorbed by yourself
Who fashions the whole. My innermost part, my Jewel, my Heart
Soul of my soul.

The rose tears open its clothes
Because of you.
The narcissus sighs, with love in its eyes
Because of you. The orchards shoot, swelling with fruit
My ever fresh garden, for you.

One moment desire brands me like fire
For you.
Another it's as though, with you I go
To a garden's cool. To open my sight, you show me God's light
Like a falcon unseeled.

/CONTINUED OVERLEAF

PERSIAN: RUMI

پوشیده چون جان می‌روی اندر میانِ جانِ من

سروِ خرامانِ منی ای رونقِ بستانِ من

چون می‌روی بی من مرو ای جانِ جان، بی تن مرو

وز چشمِ من بیرون مشو، ای مشعلِ تابانِ من

هفت آسمان را بردرم، وز هفت دریا بگذرم

چون دلبرانه بنگری در جانِ سرگردانِ من

تا آمدی اندر برم، شد کفر و ایمان چاکرم

ای دیدنِ تو دینِ من وی رویِ تو ایمانِ من

بی پا و سر کردی مرا بی خواب و خور کردی مرا

در پیشِ یعقوب اندرآ ای یوسفِ کنعانِ من

از لطفِ تو چون جان شدم وز خویشتن پنهان شدم

ای هستِ تو پنهان شده در هستیِ پنهانِ من

گل جامه در از دستِ تو وی چشم نرگس مستِ تو

ای شاخه‌ها آبستِ تو وی باغ بی پایانِ من

یک لحظه داغم می‌کشی یک دم به باغم می‌کشی

پیشِ چراغم می‌کشی تا واشود چشمانِ من

O soul above every soul
To me.
Deeper than all the depths
To me. More precious than all time
You are mine, you are mine.

Since the soul must outlive body's dust
Have no fear
Nor do I pine, aching to find
A heavenly sphere. Here or above, to keep your love
Is my only care.

Remembering the scent, of my loved one absent
I am sick to the heart,
Without my King, my being's spring
I have no part. Without your touch, loving you so much
My world is dark.

My soul is afloat, adrift like a mote
Seen in your sun.
Without you to warm me, why, why should I be
Anyone? You who designed me, essence and mind,
Have made me your own.

Royal Salah ud-Din, my Emperor, my King
Point me the way
You who guide me within, who needs not a thing
That is mine today. Greater than me, and all I could be
I must not make you stay.

RUMI (DIED 1273)

NOTES:
Salah ud-Din - Rumi's son-in-law and inspiration

PERSIAN: RUMI

ای جان پیش از جانها وی کان بیش از کانها

ای آن بیش از آنها ای آنِ من ای آنِ من

چون منزلِ ما خاک نیست گر تن بریزد باک نیست

اندیشه‌ام افلاک نیست ای وصلِ تو کیوانِ من

بر یادِ رویِ ماهِ من باشد فغان و آهِ من

بر بویِ شاهنشاهِ من هر لحظه حیرانِ من

ای جان چو ذرّه در هوا تا شد ز خورشیدت جدا

بی تو چرا باشد؟ چرا؟ ای اصلِ چهار ارکانِ من

ای شه صلاح الدینِ من ره دانِ من ره بینِ من

ای فارغ از تمکینِ من ای برتر از امکانِ من

I rejoice in the world because of this:
Because the world comes rejoicing from God.
I am in love with every star in the galaxies
Because the whole wide world is His.

O my friend, count it a joy
That Christ-like first breath of each day.
Perhaps it will bring your dried heart to life,
Because that breath is His.

The stars in the heavens do not own it,
Nor can even the angels gain it,
The secret in man's heart.
God made it, it is His.

I will drink poison as if sweet wine,
Since it is a God-like one who pours it.
From him I willingly accept the pain,
Because the healing also is His.

If my wound will not stop bleeding,
This still will be a healing.
My searing hurt is happy and blessed
Because the cool relief is His.

For the wise, what difference is there
Between states of sorrow and joy?
O cup-bearer, give me wine to declare
That love's sorrow comes from Him.

Being a King, or being poor,
For us it is all one,
Since all must bend at the sacred door
To worship in front of Him.

So Sa'di, if the flash flood that destroys
Sweeps away this suffering world,
Be brave at heart because the joys
Of heaven are firm with Him.

MUSLIH AL-DIN SA'DI (DIED 1292)
DIVAN

NOTES:
Sa'di - pen-name after royal patron

PERSIAN: MUSLIH AL-DIN SA'DI

به جهان خرّم از آنم که جهان خرّم از اوست
عاشقم بر همه عالم که همه عالم از اوست
بغنیمت شمر ایدوست دم عیسیِ صبح
تا دلِ مُرده مَگر زنده کنی کاین دم از اوست
نه فلک راست مسلّم نه ملک را حاصل
آنچه در سرِّ سویدایِ بنی‌آدم از اوست
بحلاوت بخورم زهر که شاهد ساقیست
بارادت ببرم درد که درمان هم از اوست
زخمِ خونینم اگر به نشود به باشد
خخک آن زخم که هر لحظه مرا مرهم از اوست
غم و شادی بر عارف چه تفاوت دارد؟
ساقیا باده بده شادیِ آن کاین غم از اوست
پادشاهی و گدایی بر ما یکسانست
که برین در همه را پشتِ عبادت خم از اوست
سعدیا گر بکنَد سیلِ فنا خانه‌ی دل
دل قوی دار که بُنیادِ بقا محکم از اوست

Joseph, who was lost, will come back to Canaan. Do not grieve.
This hut of sorrows one day will blaze with roses. Do not grieve.

Your troubled heart will heal, so don't let sorrow poison it,
And your desolate brain find balance. Do not grieve.

If, for whole days, the circling heavens defy our wishes,
Remember time cannot be changeless. Do not grieve.

When spring brings life to the meadow's edge, you, sweet bird,
Will draw the rose's parasol to shield your head. So do not grieve.

Don't despair that you don't know all secret mysteries,
Behind the veil more tricks lie hidden. Do not grieve.

If on foot you cross the desert, thirsting for the Ka'ba,
Though the camel-thorn may lash you, do not grieve.

God knows our mood, when mocked and love-forsaken:
He knows, who shapes all moods. So do not grieve.

O my heart, though the flash flood wipes out all life,
Noah navigates for us. Despite the tempest, do not grieve.

Though this part of our journey is so dangerous, and the goal remote,
No roads are without endings. Do not grieve.

O Hafez, in this corner of poverty, in the quietness of dark nights,
So long as your thought is prayer, your lesson the Holy Book, never grieve.

SHAMS-AL-DIN MUHAMMAD HAFEZ (DIED 1389)
DIVAN

NOTES:
Hafez - memoriser of the Qur'an
Joseph, Jacob - lost son and his father as in Torah and Qur'an stories
Noah - his ark survived the Flood

PERSIAN: SHAMS-AL-DIN MUHAMMAD HAFEZ

یوسفِ گم گشته باز آید بکنعان: غم مخور!

کلبهٔ احزان شود روزی گلستان: غم مخور!

این دلِ غمدیده حالش به شود: دل بد مکن!

وین سرِ شوریده باز آید بسامان: غم مخور!

دورِ گردون گر دو روزی بمرادِ ما نگشت

دائماً یکسان نماند حالِ دوران: غم مخور!

گر بهارِ عمر باشد باز بر طرفِ چمن

چترِ گل بر سر کشی ای مرغ خوش خوان: غم مخور!

هان مشو نومید چون واقف نه‌ای ز اسرارِ غیب:

باشد اندر پرده بازیهایِ پنهان: غم مخور!

در بیابان گر بشوقِ کعبه خواهی زد قدم

سرزنشها گر کند خارِ مغیلان: غم مخور!

حالِ ما در فرقتِ جانان و ابرامِ رقیب

جمله میداند خدایِ حال گردان: غم مخور!

ای دل ار سیلِ فنا بنیادِ هستی برکند

چون ترا نوح است کشتیبان: ز طوفان غم مخور!

گرچه منزل بس خطرناکست و مقصد بس بعید:

هیچ راهی نیست کانرا نیست پایان: غم مخور!

حافظا در کنجِ فقر و خلوتِ شبهایِ تار

تا بود وردت دعا و درسِ قرآن: غم مخور!

Don't delude yourself that you
Are arriving close to God
As you've never escaped yourself
Where could you have gone?

Though your head may scrape the stars,
Don't be deceived in pride.
You remain the self-same handful of dust:
Swept upwards on the wind.

With all your innate bone-headedness,
Don't be led astray,
For just as your flame begins to dance
Your candle gutters away.

Smash the glass of your self-conceit:
Don't polish it a thousandth time.
However brilliant the mirror becomes,
Shows baseness not the sublime.

Devotion's true confidence
Comes from soaring above desire,
Whereas in your self conceit
You lift empty hands in prayer.

My broken body is weak and drained,
So visit me, wish me health:
You will reach a suffering painful heart
When you reach myself.

You may long cackle in the flame,
And sing and dance in riot:
Go rue seeds, leave me alone
Tonight I seek only quiet.

No song, no fluttering hearts,
No bubbling ecstasy:
In heaven's vintage wine
Yours lacks maturity.

/CONTINUED OVERLEAF

PERSIAN: ABDUL QADER BIDEL

نبری گمان که یعنی بخدا رسیده باشی!
تو ز خود نرفته بیرون: بکجا رسیده باشی؟
سرت ار بچرخ ساید: نخوری فریبِ عزّت
که همان کفِّ غباری بهوا رسیده باشی
بهوایِ خود سریها نروی زره که چون شمع
سرِ ناز تا ببالد تهِ پا رسیده باشی
زدنِ آینه بسنگت ز هزار صیقل اولی
که بزشتیِٔ جهانی ز جلّا رسیده باشی
خمِ طرّه یِ اجابت بعُروجِ بی نیازیست
تو بوهمِ خویش دستی بدعا رسیده باشی
همه تن شکستِ رنگیم: مگذار ز پرسشِ ما
که بدردِ دل رسیدی چوبها رسیده باشی
برو ای سپند امشب سرو برگِ ما خموشیست!
تو که سوختند و سازت: بنوا رسیده باشی
نه ترنّمی نه وجدی نه طپیدنی نه جوشی
بخُمِ سپهر تا کی میِٔ نارسیده باشی؟

You have not studied the world:
Take one step out of yourself.
You must transcend yourself
To reach anywhere else.

As your body wearies and fades, Bidel,
Let this be sufficient grace,
That you reach a discerning ear
Like a distant echo's trace.

ABDUL QADER BIDEL (DIED 1721)
DIVAN

PERSIAN: ABDUL QADER BIDEL

نگهِ جهان نَوَردی؟ قدمی ز خود برون آ!
که ز خویش اگر گذشتی: همه جا رسیده باشی
ز شکستِ رنگِ هستی اثَر تو بیدل این بس
که بگوشِ امتیازی چو صدا رسیده باشی

Turkish

Turkish is spoken from Western China through Central Asia to Anatolia and the Balkans by an estimated 60 to 90 million people. Turks penetrated the greater Iranian world as nomadic herdsmen and military conscripts, as well as ambassadors from the independent Buddhist kingdoms, and were present in Central Asia already by the 6th century. This pattern continued after the 7th century Arab Islamic conquests, with Turkish slave soldiers forming the caliphal guard in Baghdad and Samarra. From 1000 AD the Turkish Islamic dynasty of Ghazni (in Afghanistan) began military incursions into the Indian Hindu world; this established a pattern of an ethnically Turkish military aristocracy carrying the religion of Islam and the literary language of Persia that would be repeated till the 18th century. In 1050 the Seljuq Turks established an empire based on Isfahan and Marv, with a collateral branch conquering Byzantine Anatolia in 1071 with their regional capital at Konya. Administrative and literary activities were carried on in Persian until after the Mongol victory at Köse Daq in 1243, which led to more intensive Turkification in Azerbaijan and Anatolia. In 1277 the Karaman ruler declared Turkish the official language of the state. It was during this period that Rumi's son Sultan Veled presided over the translation of Rumi's original Persian works into Turkish.

Yunus Emre

The first great poet of Turkish, the mystic Yunus Emre composed his poetry in the folk style, using the 'dortluq' quatrains with refrain. His Sufi poetry was written to be sung, and he belongs to the tradition of the Babas, who were themselves closely related to the bakhshis and shamans of the pre-Islamic tradition. His poetry in the 'oghuz' western Turkish vernacular had retained its universal appeal, speaking directly to ordinary people and transcending artificial differences of class, colour and creed.

Your love has taken me from me
It is you I need, only you
Day in, day out, I burn
It is you I need, only you

Neither plenty makes me rejoice
Nor dearth complain
Your love consoles me
It is you I need, only you

Your love kills lovers
Love plunges them into the sea
They are filled with this epiphany
It is you I need, only you

I drink your love's wine
Crazed, I wander the hills
Day in, day out, I think of you
It is you I need, only you

Sufis seek spiritual companionship
Akhis seek the hereafter
Crazed lovers, like Majnun, seek Leila
It is you I need, only you

If they kill me
Scatter my ashes to the sky
If earth calls me in a moment
It is you I need, only you

My name is Yunus
My fire increases day by day
My aim in the two worlds (here and hereafter)
Is you, I need only you

YUNUS EMRE (DIED CIRCA 1320)

NOTES:
Sufis - mystical Muslims
Akhis - mystical Tukish Muslims, dedicated to the service of others, especially offering hospitality
    to travellers (c.f. Travels of Ibn Battuta)
Majnun - literally 'possessed by Jinn', Arab lover, crazed for love of Leila
Leila - Arab beloved, from a different tribe than Majnun
Yunus - the Prophet Jonah, name of the poet

TURKISH: YUNUS EMRE

Aşkın aldı benden beni
Bana seni gerek seni
Ben yanarım dünü günü
Bana seni gerek seni

Ne varlığa sevinirim
Ne yokluğa yerinirim
Aşkın ile avunurum
Bana seni gerek seni

Aşkın asıklar öldürür
Aşk denizine daldırır
Tecelli ile doldurur
Bana seni gerek seni

Aşkın şarabından içem
Mecnun olup dağa düşem
Sensin dün-ü gün endişem
Bana seni gerek seni

Sofulara sohbet gerek
Ahilere ahret gerek
Mecnunlara Leyla gerek
Bana seni gerek seni

Eğer beni öldüreler
Külüm göğe savuralar
Topragım anda çagıra
Bana seni gerek seni

Yunus'dur benim adım
Gün geldikçe artar odum
Iki cihanda maksudum
Bana seni gerek seni

Punjabi

The number of Punjabi speakers has been estimated variously as anywhere between 25 to 57 million, and even up to 100 million; it is spoken from Delhi to Kashmir to Multan to Peshawar in north-west India and Pakistan, as well as in a worldwide diaspora. It belongs to the Indian sub-family of the Indo-European language family and has many features of vocabulary and structure common with Sanskrit and Persian, as well as shading off into its neighbouring dialects, Seraiki, Pahari and Hindko. Islam came to the Punjab with the conquests of Mahmud of Ghazni in the early 11th century, who terminated the rule of the Hindu Rajas of Kabul, the Salt Range and Lahore. There may have been earlier contacts with the already established Muslim areas of Sindh to the south, which had already come within the orbit of Islam by the 8th century. One of the religious luminaries of the earliest phase of Islam in the Punjab was the Ghaznavid Hujwiri, who wrote an extensive Sufi treatise in Persian, and who is still venerated as 'Data Ganj-Bakhsh' in Lahore.

Shaikh Farid

The first writer of Punjabi poetry was Shaikh or 'Baba' Farid who was granted by the 13th century Turkish Tughluq dynasty of Delhi a landholding at Ajudhan (Pakpattan), a major river crossing on the route from Afghanistan to Delhi. Known as 'Ganj-e Shekar' – treasure of sugar, Shaikh Farid used his poetry to transmit the teachings of the Chishti Sufi confraternity and also meant it to be sung by shrine singers known as 'qawwal'. His shrine to this day boasts one of the finest 'qawwali' ensembles of the Indo Muslim world. His message of earthly and divine love, simple humanity, honesty and rejection of hypocrisy, and the desire to reach higher levels of spiritual consciousness, spoke to a wide audience, and his shrine was a focus for the conversion to Islam of the Jat and Rajput tribes of the Punjab over several centuries. His verses are preserved in the 1604 recension of the hymns and teachings of Guru Nanak, who included these Sufi Muslim poems in the Gurmukhi script in the central scripture of the Sikhs. (The Sikhs originated in the Punjab in the 15th century and took military and political power there from 1801 until the British imperial conquest of 1849.)

Shah Husain

In the Moghul period, one of the students at Shaikh Farid's shrine was Shah Husain, the son of a weaver, whose ecstatic behaviour scandalised Muslims and Hindus alike. His high learning and intense love attracted the young Brahmin Madho Lal, with whom he lies buried in Lahore. In the poem quoted, Husain dramatises himself as the Punjabi folk-heroine Heer who finds no helper to help her cross the river to join her beloved Ranjha – this symbolising the long and painful journey of the soul.

Bullhe Shah

Deriving high prestige from his descent from the Prophet Muhammad, Sayyid 'Abdullah, from Uchch, was popularly known as Bullhe Shah. Uchch is one of the spiritual centres of Sufism in the Punjab, settled by Sufis and scholars throughout the middle ages. This poem, 'Terey Ishq nechaya...' dates from his youth, when he had inadvertently angered his master, and resorted to a transvestite dance to make his master laugh and forgive him. Bullhe Shah's life and poetry were not written down until the late 19th century. It was from the lineage of his shrine musicians at Kasur that the royal musicians of Kabul were recruited in the early 19th century – and the current generation of that family provided the music to end this feast of Sufi poetry and song.

O Farid!
If you have such fine wisdom,
do not denounce others so quickly.
Lower your gaze and
think about what is inside your
        own clothing.

O Farid!
They shriek and shout
and always offer their advice.
They have been seduced by Satan,
how can they concentrate on counting
        their prayer-beads?

PUNJABI: SHAIKH FARID

فریدا!
جے توں عقلِ لطیف
کالے لِکھ نہ لیکھ
اپڑے گریباں میں
سِر نیواں کر کے دیکھ

فریدا!
گو کیندیاں چا نگیندیاں
مَتیّں دیندیاں نِت
جو شیطان ونجایا
سو کِت پھیرے چِت

O Farid!
The lane is muddy, the house is far away
and I have a commitment to my love.
If I set out, my cloak will be soiled,
If I stay, my commitment will be broken.
So, let my cloak be drenched and muddied,
O God, let the clouds burst.
Let me go and meet Him,
Let my love be not disgraced.

O Farid!
Serve the Lord and cleanse your heart,
Saints must embody the resilience of trees.

PUNJABI: SHAIKH FARID

فریدا!

گلیئے چکڑ دور گھر

نال پیارے نیہو

چلاں تاں بھجے کمبلی

رہاں تاں ٹٹے نیہو

بھجو سجو کمبلی

اللہ ورسأو میہو

جاءِ ملاں تنہاں سجناں

ٹٹے عُنا ہیں نیہو

فریدا!

صاحِب دی کر چاکری

دِل وی لاہ بھرانِد

درویشاں نوں لوڑیئے

رُکھاں دی جیرانِد

O Farid!
I am dressed from head to toe
in pious black.
I wander around, full of sin,
yet people call me Saint!

O Farid,
I thought I was alone in my pain,
but the whole world is suffering.
When I look down from the roof,
I see the same fire in every house

SHAIKH FARID (DIED 1266)
AS RECORDED IN ADI GRANTH COMPILED 1604

PUNJABI: SHAIKH FARID

فریدا!
کالے میں ڈھے کپڑے
کالا میں ڈھا ویس
گنہی بھریا میں پھراں
لوک کہے درویش

فریدا!
میں جانیاں دُکھ مُجھ کوں
دُکھ سیائیٔ جگ
اُچے چڑھ کے دیکھیا
گھر گھر ایہا آگ

I too must go to Ranjha's dwelling
Someone please come with me
I beg, I plead, on my knees
But I have to go alone

> The river is deep, the raft is ancient
> Lions stalk the banks
> If someone would bring me word of my beloved
> I would give them the rings off my fingers

By night I suffer, by day I am sick
The agonies of love are fresh and raw
My body is wracked with strange pain.
My beloved Ranjha is famed as a healer

> The worthless faqir Husein says, the Lord is sending messages...

SHAH HUSAIN (DIED 1599)

NOTES:
Ranjha - punjabi hero, beloved of Heer

PUNJABI: SHAH HUSAIN

میں بھی جھوک رانجھن دی جاناں، نال میرے کوئی چلّے

پَیراں پوندی، مِنّتاں کردی، جاناں تاں پیا اِکلّے !

نیں بھی ڈونگھی، تلاءُ اناشیں نہاں تاں تِتن مَلّے

جے کوئی خبر متراں دی لیاوے، ہتھ دینی آں چھلّے

راتیں درد، وِینہاں در ماندی، گھاؤ متراں دے اَلّھے

رانجھن یار، طبیب سنیدا، میں تن درد اوتّے

کہے حسین فقیر نمانا، سائیں سنیہوڑے گھلّے

Your love has set up camp in me
Of my own free will, I drank this cupful of poison
Come back quickly, o healer, or I will die
Your love has made me dance to its beat

The sun has hidden itself, the red glow remains
I would sacrifice myself if you would reveal yourself again
I have committed a grave error by not going with you
Your love has made me dance to its beat

Do not hold me back, o mother, from this love
The boat is going into the rapids, who can pull it back?
My senses had abandoned me when I went off with the boatmen
Your love has made me dance to its beat

In this jungle of love, the peacock speaks
I see in my beautiful beloved both Qibla and Ka'ba
Having wounded me so, he has never sought news of my condition.
Your love has made me dance to its beat

O Bullhe! The Lord has brought me to Inayat's door
And he has dressed me in the red and green garb of the faqir
Wherever I stamp my dancing heel, there I find the same old Him
Your love has made me dance to its beat

BULLHE SHAH (DIED 1758)
- AS PRESERVED BY KASUR SHRINE SINGERS

NOTES:
Qibla - the direction of Muslim prayer
Ka'ba - the cube at Mecca
Bullhe - a diminutive of Abdullah in Punjabi
Inayat - the poet's spiritual master

PUNJABI: BULLHE SHAH

تیرے عشق نچائیاں کر تھیّا تھیّا!

تیرے عشق نے ڈیرا میرے اندر کیتا، بھر کے زہر پیالہ میں تاں آپے پیتا
جھبدے بوہڑیں وے طبیبا، نہیں تے میں مر گئیّا
تیرے عشق نچائیاں کر تھیّا تھیّا!

چھپ گیا وے سورج، باہر رہ گئی آ لالی، وے میں صدقے ہوواں دیویں مُڑ جے وکھالی
پیرا! میں بھل گئیّاں، تیرے نال نہ گئیّا
تیرے عشق نچائیاں کر تھیّا تھیّا!

ایس عشقے دے کولوں سینیوں ہٹک نہ مائے، لاہو جاندڑے بیڑے کیہڑا موڑ لیائے
میری عقل جو بھلی، نال مُہانیاں دے گئیّا
تیرے عشق نچائیاں کر تھیّا تھیّا!

ایس عشقے دی جھنگی وچ مور بولیندا، سانوں قبلے تے کعبہ سوہنایار دسیندا
سانوں گھائل کر کے، پھر خبر نہ لیندا
تیرے عشق نچائیاں کر تھیّا تھیّا!

بلھا! شوہ نے آندا مینوں عنایت دے بوہے، جس نے مینوں پوائے چولے ساوے تے سوہے
جاں میں ماری ہے اڈی، مل پیا ہے وہیّا
تیرے عشق نچائیاں کر تھیّا تھیّا!

Sufism 69

ACKNOWLEDGMENTS

'Putting creativity into the hands of clients'

Axon Publishing

This unique publication has been designed and produced by
Axon Publishing, a publishing agency that creates customer
magazines, catalogues, business-to-business and other
communications in partnership with a range of corporate clients
WWW.AXONPUBLISH.COM

A&B
Arts & Business New Partners
working together

FONTS
Latin: ITC Galliard
Arabic: DecoType Thuluth
Persian/Farsi: Lotus Linotype
Punjabi: Noori Nastaliq